Has Our Faith Changed?

Reflections On the Faith
for Today's Adult Christian

René Laurentin

Has Our Faith Changed?

Reflections On the Faith for Today's Adult Christian

alba house

A DIVISION OF THE SOCIETY OF ST. PAUL
STATEN ISLAND, NEW YORK 10314

Translator: Sister Mary Dominic

Original Italian Edition published by Le Edizioni Paoline, Rome, Italy under the title **Dio Dopo La Morte Di Dio.**

Nihil Obstat:
Daniel V. Flynn, J.C.D.

Imprimatur:
Joseph P. O'Brien, S.T.D.
Vicar General, Archdiocese of New York
June 28, 1971

Library of Congress Catalog Card Number: 71-169146

ISBN: 0-8189-0238-8

CONTENTS

The symptoms—The development and the paradox of theologies of the death of God—"The death of God" according to tradition—"The death of God" according to the enemies of God—Are Christians responsible for atheism?—The death of God is the death of man—Christian theologians of "the death of God."

A formidable mutation—The earth is no longer the center of our world—We are older than we used to think—Our heart is in question—Do not sacrifice the substance for the shadow—The synod's conclusions—Faith is simple.

A folly—A dark and luminous cloud—How God speaks to each of us—How are we

HAS OUR FAITH CHANGED?

The Crisis of Faith

1 THE CRISIS OF FAITH

The Catholic faith is questioned today in two different ways. On the one hand there are new demands, positive and constructive, arising from the Council: that the faith should be more closely in accord with the word of God, the Gospel; that it should be more involved in the reality of the world as it is; that it should adapt itself to contemporary language and to the problems posed at depth by the mentality of modern times. On the other hand, the faith is suffering a sort of "negative crisis," as if it no longer knew where it was. Certain dogmatic formulas are contested, doubted or at least regarded as relative. Hence a certain confusion.

Let us begin our reflections by analyzing this crisis. It is perhaps taking a risk to attack the problem from this negative point of view. The man who shouts 'Fire' in a crowd provokes confusion and sometimes lethal accidents. And when someone talks about an epidemic everyone takes his pulse and feels ill—even those who are quite well. . . . So we have to be careful on this point.

But we should not be afraid to face the question, including its difficult and its depressing aspects. Paul VI has asked us to do so. On March 29, 1967, when he announced to the bishops of the entire world the five

2

point agenda of their conference, he formulated as the first point: *"the dangers which threaten the faith and the diverse forms of atheism."*

The faith today does encounter difficulties. All of us are more or less conscious of them, and ask ourselves: Why has a faith which was perhaps rather facile, implanted from childhood like a good habit, been so shaken, and sometimes troubled? Why is it so hard to see its relevance in our lives? Why is it so often something vague and fluctuating and not the force which animated the early Christians, and involved them totally as individuals, in a common life. Are we suffering from some sort of plague, a spiritual sickness peculiar to our time? Or is it perhaps a crisis of growth?

This last hypothesis is a sound one. The synod of bishops recognized it, in October 1967. But every crisis of growth can become melodramatic, when those who suffer it do not understand what is happening to them. They can think themselves ill and acquire a complex about their illness. That is what we have to avoid.

Let us not be afraid either of words or of realities. For we are strong in the gift of God, in the resurrection of Christ which began in us at our baptism and which comes to its fruition in the Church as spring does in the apparent death of winter. And we are strong too in our sharing in the vast effort at renewal which the Church dared to undertake at the Council, counting on an effort from every Christian, increasingly aware and increasingly committed. So let us understand what

The paradoxical and much
publicized expression,
"The Death of God," covers
a wide range of diverse
theories, some good and
some bad. The worst, the
atheistic, would do away
altogether with the idea of
God. The best would do
away with certain simplistic
ideas of God and would
try to rediscover God in other
ways more worthy of him.
But God is not dead. He is
very much alive. He is
life itself. Only a lively faith
in this fact can overcome
the world.

has happened to us, as it happened to St. Peter, as he walked on the sea.

What is this "crisis of faith" then, that everyone is talking about today? What is its origin, and where is it leading us and how are we to remedy it?

THE SYMPTOMS

Let us start with an attempt at diagnosis: what are the symptoms of this crisis? This first chapter is concerned with considering a strange phenomenon, a phenomenon which takes even stranger forms in many Christian countries, but a phenomenon which is instructive as well as striking: the rise and development of what are called "theologies of the death of God."

The expression itself is paradoxical, for *theo-logy,* even according to the etymology of the word, is the science of God, in Greek *Theos.* When then theology talks about the death of God, it seems to be denying its own end and object. As far back as the eleventh century St. Anselm attacked this contradiction in principle in the course of his meditation on Psalm 52: "The fool has said in his heart, there is no God." God is Being which exists of itself, *a se,* necessarily, remarks St. Anselm, and to say that necessary Being does not exist is a contradiction in terms. That is why the psalmist calls anyone who offers us propositions of this sort a fool. "He contradicts himself and condemns himself."

The fool today says "God is dead." But God does not die. He is the absolute Living One. He is Life itself. He who pronounces this kind of verdict is a fool, like his predecessor in the eleventh century. And as for the theologian of the death of God, he denies his own title, as if he called himself a hair-dresser for the bald or a chiropodist for those who have no feet.

But let us look at the matter a little more closely: it is never a good thing to get rid of a wide-spread idea by caricaturing it. One can rid oneself of the idea, but that does not dispose of the problem which underlies it.

The fact that so curiously absurd a formula could become so popular in America, in Holland and in many other countries, that it could make its way in circles which are representative both of the younger generation, and of the young middle-aged, is a sign of the times. I was struck, for instance, at receiving a message at Christmas from a group of Catholic students which said: "For us the great adventure of Christmas is the death of God . . . the God invented by men to answer for the mysteries of nature, for the 'established order' and for evil. It is a byword that as man's knowledge grows, God's territory shrinks . . . but on the other hand, we are in the process of discovering the meaning of the words of Christ and of St. Paul, the meaning of the Bible, and even the meaning of a good many religious concepts elaborated by theologians."

"The death of God": this paradoxical and much publicized formula covers theories which are diverse enough, ranging from the worst to the best—the worst, those which deny God, the atheistical theories; the best, those which witness to the fact that a certain *simpliste* idea of God is dead, and that it is necessary to rediscover God in a way which is less unworthy of him.

"The death of God" according to tradition

The formula "God is dead" is an ancient one. In Christian tradition it denotes the drama of Calvary, the death of Christ, God made man, in his human nature, to save us. It is love which involves God in death: "God dies in order to live in you," an old German carol used to sing.

"The death of God" according to the enemies of God

In Europe, at the beginning of the nineteenth century, "the death of God" took the form of a strange and vertiginous myth. The theme first appeared in Jean-Paul Richter's romantic dream popularized by Madame de Staël (*De l'Allemagne,* 1810). It is in a churchyard, a little before midnight. The graves open and the shades of the dead appear. They summon Christ, and he answers:

"There is no God . . . we are all orphans. Neither you nor I have a father any more."

There are analogous dreams to be found in Gérard de Nerval and Heinrich Heine. "Nothing can save him," writes Heine, "Don't you hear the sound of the bell? Get on your knees. They are taking the sacraments to a dying God."

This myth expressed the presentiment of a new world, where God is losing his former place and tends to vanish in the hearts of men. Among the social reformers, the myth became structural. God for Feuerbach, one of the inspirers of Marx, is alienation, and the death of God is the liberation of enslaved man. The myth took its most aggressive form in Nietzsche in *Zarathustra,* where the last man announces that God is dead and Nietzsche celebrates .the news. More than that, he wants himself to be an actor in the play, an accomplice in the assassination. For him the death of God is the liberation of man; it prepares the way for the birth of the super-man. The underlying idea is that God can live only in human consciousness and the human conscience, where he is an undesirable guest: "he is a thought which makes crooked what is straight." The atheism of the nineteenth century is a form of humanism. It wants the death of God in order that man may live.

ARE CHRISTIANS
RESPONSIBLE FOR ATHEISM?

This myth, alas, has been inspired to a large extent by false presentations of religion and of Christianity itself, narrow, oppressive, conventional, at the service

10

of interests foreign to Christ and to the Gospel. So Voltaire, anti-clerical as he was, used to receive the Sacrament at Easter in the midst of his peasant tenantry in the chapel of his country-house at Fernay, in order to maintain the "principles" which assured him of the conscientious submission of the unfortunate people he exploited. Men have been oppressed at times in the name of "Christian morals" understood in a sense foreign to the message of Christ. And this is not ancient history. We have only to think of Latin America. A great many bishops there, especially in Chile, have witnessed to the Gospel in a liberating way, giving the lands of the Church to facilitate agrarian reform and overcome want. But others have blocked agrarian reform in the name of "the Christian ethic of the right of property." As late as 1963, when the Brazilian authorities attempted cautious requisitions of land left uncultivated by large land-owners, certain prelates declared that a Christian had no right to accept them. A Chilean bishop, Msgr. Pinera Carvallo, declared plainly at the synod (on October 7, 1967) that errors of this sort were the determining cause of the "crisis of faith" in Latin America:

"In our continent, atheism arises from feelings and living conditions rather than from ideas.

"Among us secularization has been, and still remains, a reaction on the part of the middle class which has recently arrived at wealth and power, not against God but against the Catholic Church, which appears to it to be socially compromised with the aristocracy, and with it to retain power and wealth and culture in a *milieu* to which the middle class is barred. Anti-clericalism preceded atheism. The secularists have ended by ceasing to believe in God.

"The same is true of Marxism. Our people, our intellectuals, our students, are not drawn to Marxism *because* it is atheistic but *although* it is atheistic. They are looking for a way of changing economic and social structures, and they find in Marxism a coherent system which produces results, a theory which involves a 'praxis,' by means of a method animated by a *mystique*. The Church, on the other hand, appears to them to be incapable of making any effective change even in the mentality and structural thinking of its own experts. In due course they lose confidence, and turn to Marxism, and by way of Marxism, without explicitly wanting to do so, to atheism.

"The most useful thing today is not to point out errors, but to free ourselves from the incubus of certain customs, and in absolute fidelity to the Gospel to involve ourselves wholeheartedly in the contemporary world."

On the 8th of October Msgr. Carraro, bishop of Verona, expressed similar views concerning the industrial situation in modern Europe. What he said in substance was that industrialism is a progress, as Paul VI recognized in *Populorum progressio,* but that nevertheless it implies a risk, the risk of becoming a process of depersonalization. Man is being absorbed by economic and technological values. Workers are becoming machines or simply wheels in machines, deprived of personality. Man is being sacrificed to the iron law of production, and this is one of the elements which constitute atheism in practice.

The theme of "the death of God" then, as it appears in Nietzsche and the social reformers of the nineteenth century, implies a lesson for us. It invites us to take the Gospel and its demands on us seriously, to take seriously the message of liberation so clearly announced by St. Paul. The real message of Christ does not paralyze either thought or action in the service of truth and justice, or in the service of progress and the research which it implies. On the contrary it exalts them. If we, who bear the name of "Christians" or "Christian nations," betray this message in our lives, we kill God in the hearts of men and peoples. There is a risk that the drama which is being played out in countries like France, which have "lost the working class," will be reproduced on an international scale, for the "rich nations" are the Christian nations, and they have not been able to solve the problem of underdeveloped countries. More than that, the iron law of economics produces degrading terms of exchange and keeps certain peoples in a permanent state of underdevelopment and poverty. Such is the case of Brazil for example. There is no question here of accusing this or that group or nation, but rather of shouldering, each one of us, our own responsibilities, domestic, professional, political or ecclesiastical, in such a way as to make manifest in our words and actions the God who liberates and not a caricature of him. We are the image of God for those who do not believe in him. Let us be so in spirit and in truth. It is a heavy responsibility. It was to assume this responsibility that Paul VI wrote *Populorum progressio*.

THE DEATH OF GOD IS THE DEATH OF MAN

"The death of God" as Nietzsche saw it carries another lesson for us. Indeed this theme has engendered another in the very society in which it was born. "The death of God" involves "the death of man," diagnosed by structuralism. M. Michel Foucault, the structuralist philosopher, ends his book *Les Mots et les Choses*:

14

"Man is an invention of which the archeology of our thought clearly indicates the recent date, and perhaps the imminent end."

In other words, man has exalted himself in denying the transcendence of God. But he has been like the woodman who saws off the branch on which he is sitting. His liberation has taken the form of a free fall. M. Michel Foucault recognizes this consequence elsewhere:

"In our day it is not so much the absence or death of God which is affirmed but the end of man ... the death of God and the end of man are in part bound up together. ... According to Nietzsche it is the last man who announces that he has killed God. But since he has killed God, it is he himself who must answer for his own finiteness. ... More than the death of God, or rather in the wake of this death, and according to a correlation at depth with it, what the thought of Nietzsche announces is the end of his murderer."

Sometime before M. Michel Foucault, Roger Martin de Gard had already grasped this connection. One of the characters in his novel *L'Été 1914* has said already:

"Nietzsche disposed of the notion of God. He put in its place the notion of man. That is nothing, it is just the first stage. Atheism must now go much further, it must get rid too of the idea of man."

Yes, to kill God is to kill man too. If Hitler was a man who was, according to Nietzsche, liberated, he is also the symbol of one of the multitudinous ways in which "the death of God" involves the death of men: for millions of soldiers, for millions of Jews, for Hitler himself, in the apocalyptic ruins of Berlin.

CHRISTIAN THEOLOGIANS OF "THE DEATH OF GOD"

But the "theology of the death of God" which people talk about today is not that of Nietzsche; for Nietzsche was anti-Christian and intended to construct not a theology but an anti-theology, an atheistic humanism.

The "new theologies" are the constructions of Christians anxious to live the Gospel, at the outset the work of certain American Protestants. What has struck them

16

is that a certain image of God is going, the image of a narrow and *simpliste* religion, and that it is not a question of conserving this image—the image criticized by Feuerbach, but of going beyond it. Their criticism is directed specially against a certain "American religion," flourishing but superficial, and regarded as above reproach. This religion provides an alibi for the demands of the Gospel rather than a realization of them. It looks for a conventional security from a God who is a kind of Eternal Life Insurance, in exchange for a few observances and a number of dollars, without any great connection with the life of God. What is positive in the theologians of "the death of God" is that they want to derive God from the source of the Gospel, not fabricate "a little religious world," not keep alive in the secular world little islands of religiosity like "Indian reserves," but rather try to live the Gospel in this secular world itself, and work towards realizing there peace and justice, self-giving and brotherhood among men. Their positive element might be summed up in the refrain of the breviary: "God is love, and he who lives in love lives in God and God in him" (even if he is not consciously aware of it).

But the critique of these theologians sometimes goes to dangerous lengths. In renouncing structures, dogmas and institutions, they go as far as losing any sense of God's objective reality, any sense of the Godhead of Christ. They see in the Christ of the Gospel the man who reveals to them the best of themselves, but not the God made man in order to save them. A sense of the Incarnation and a sense of transcendence vanish together. Only man is left. This is what has happened in the thinking of Professor Van Buren or Professor Altizer or Professor Hamilton, and even in that of certain young Dutch and French Catholics who have been caught up in this current of thought.

In others, like Professor Harvey Cox or Professor Vahanian, this new and precipitous approach remains deeply Christian. Such too is the case with Dietrich Bonhoeffer, whose name these theologians invoke without attaining to his level. Bonhoeffer, moreover, is not a theologian of "the death of God." He speaks rather of "the silence of God," or of a sort of "weakness of God" in line with the Incarnation. He used to like to quote that passage from the Gospel according to St. Matthew (8, 17): "He took on himself our infirmities and bore our sicknesses."

"According to St. Matthew 8, 27," he comments, "it is clear that Christ does not bring us succor in virtue of his all-powerfulness, but in virtue of his weakness and his suffering. . . . God is weak and without power in this world, and it is precisely in this way that he is close to us and helps us."

This is in harmony with the words of Huvelin to Charles de Foucauld:

"Christ has taken the lowest place so completely that no one will ever be able to take it from him."

Bonhoeffer died a martyr in the etymological sense of the word: in *witness* to his faith in Jesus Christ. This evangelical theologian, one of the most rigorous of his communion, had every means at his disposal to escape from Hitlerism. English and American universities invited him to a life of freedom and honor. He had only to decide which offer to accept. In Germany he was forbidden to teach and his life was threatened. Yet he voluntarily put an end to his stay in England in 1935; he cut short his course of lectures in the United States in 1939. He returned to Germany. He knew what awaited him there. He was hanged by the Gestapo on Low Sunday, 1945, after celebrating Communion for the last time for his fellow-prisoners. What answers in him to the theme of "the death of God" is something which lies very deep, like "the dark night" of St. John of the Cross. It is also his own death in Jesus Christ. His doctrinal faith was unshaken, and there are few who have known how to realize in their lives to this degree the exigence of Christ.

The line which traces itself back to Bonhoeffer is unequal in value, and very diverse in direction, even in what concerns the meaning given to the expression, "the death of God." Interpretations of this range from the "mystical night" through which Bonhoeffer passed to a radical atheism which retains no more than an attachment in praxis to the message of the Gospel as an authentic way of life. God is dead in the hearts of a great many of our contemporaries, those who profess atheism and those who are atheists at heart, either by inclination or weakness, even among those who call themselves Christians. The place of God in so far as it is inscribed in the institutions of Christendom shrinks inexorably, and the more personal, more demanding way of finding God, which is imposed by the world of today, remains to be discovered.

With all its insufficiencies, its risks and its errors, the current of thought in the theologians of "the death of God" contains then lessons for us in our attempt to diagnose the crisis of faith. The lessons are these:

1. There is no doubt that the word God has been abused: it has been gratuitously degraded. We have caricatured God, as the Council plainly recognized:

"Atheism, taken as a whole, is not a spontaneous development but stems from a variety of causes, including a critical reaction against religious beliefs, and in some places against the Christian religion in particular. Hence believers can have more than a little to do with the birth of atheism. To the extent that they neglect their own training in the faith, or teach erroneous doctrine, or are deficient in their religious, moral, or social life, they must be said to conceal rather than reveal the authentic face of God and religion" (Church in the Modern World, n. 19).

"Theologies of the death of God" are to some extent a reaction against the abuse of language. In this connection we are reminded of the early Christians accused of atheism because they refused to accept the pagan gods, and answering with St. Justin, "We are atheists as far as these gods are concerned" (*Apology,* ch. 6). "If one remembers the history of the word atheism and how it has been applied, even to Spinoza," writes Merleau-Ponty, "one is forced to admit that any thought which displaces or defines otherwise what has been accepted as sacred is called atheist."

2. In a more general way we have sinned by our

formalism. Christians have put their trust in the external forms of religion, and in their lives have largely remained strangers to the demands of the Gospel and to God himself.

In a message addressed to the synod by contemplatives there is an echo at depth of the positive exigencies of the new current of thought. For a true contemplative is a man present to his time. He is aware of its life. He takes its demands upon himself, as St. Bernard did. Here then is the message read to the Synod on October 10, 1967:

"The contemplative who by his vocation has withdrawn into the desert . . . can recognize himself in the trials which are assailing certain Christians today. He understands their suffering and sees the meaning of it. He knows the dark night: 'My God, my God, why hast thou forsaken me?' (Ps 22:2; cf. Mt 27: 46). . . . The world is tempted to sink into atheism, into the negation of this God who cannot be grasped at its own level. . . . According to some, one could not even reach God, who would be by definition transcendent, totally other. . . .

"The Christian contemplative also is aware of this fundamental fact, which is rooted in mystical tradition, that the God who reveals himself to us in his Word reveals himself to us as unknown, in so far as he is inaccessible in this life to our concepts (Ex 33:20). Familiar with a God who is "absent," as if "non-existent" at a natural level, the contemplative is perhaps better able to understand the attitude of those who are not satisfied with a presentation of mystery

at the level of an object. But he knows nevertheless
that God gives himself beyond words or ideas to the
touch of the spirit which waits and is purified.

"In the same way the contemplative understands
more easily how the temptation to atheism which
attacks certain Christians can affect their faith in a
way which is in the end sound and healthy, how it is
a trial which is analogous to the "mystical nights." The
desert strips our heart bare; it carries away our pre-
texts, our alibis, our imperfect images of God; it re-
duces us to what is essential, confronts us with the
truth of ourselves without the possibility of flight.
That can be beneficial for faith itself: it is at the heart
of our poverty that the miracles of God's mercy are
manifest.

"Though it goes by the way of the desert, with
which the temptation to atheism can have a likeness,
the experience of the contemplative is not negative:
the absence of the transcendent God is also, in para-

22

doxical fashion, his immanent presence.

"The night of faith opens upon the indisplaceable assurance set in our hearts by God himself, who wished to test us. The cloistered life itself is a witness to the reality of this history. . . . We have understood how true it is that Christ has risen from the dead."

Has the Council
Changed the Faith?

II HAS THE COUNCIL CHANGED THE FAITH?

Let us go on with our attempt to diagnose the crisis of faith.

In the last chapter we were examining some of the adventurous theologies which are enjoying today a strange public success. It has taught us a lesson—that the faith must make demands on us if it is to live at all. It can no longer accommodate itself to sham or appearances. Where it remains a convention it will go. The only faith which can survive in our time is a living and exacting faith.

We shall take up our diagnostic again on ground which is more familiar. We are all conscious enough, though to different degrees, that the religious formulas to which we were accustomed are being re-examined and to some extent changed. The older ones among us feel slightly dizzy. The style of preaching has changed: sermons do not speak the same language. Catechisms go through their evolutions along with the liturgy. Some of us are disturbed about it, puzzled and confused.

So what one used to believe as "Gospel truth," doesn't one believe it any more? Has our religion, which used to be called unchanging, changed? If it did, wouldn't it be denying itself?

I met in America an old lady who was anxious about the faith of the Pope himself. She was afraid he might be contaminated by Marxism. She was the victim of some rather melodramatic propaganda—and she easily allowed herself to be reassured.

In short the faith today, to different degrees in different quarters, is under examination. It is questioned, and many think that the Council has changed the faith.

A FORMIDABLE MUTATION

This is a superficial interpretation. Certainly there has been a change without precedent. But it had begun before the Second Vatican Council. All the Council has done is abandon the tactics of the ostrich, which hides its head in the sand so as not to see the danger. It has faced the problem in order to find a solution to it. It has tried to keep an irresistible movement from losing its balance. It is not the cause of this movement but the attempt to make it healthy.

Let us see things clearly, as Paul VI asked his audience at Albano, on September 3, 1967 to do. And he gave them the key to the problem: "Let us try to see and understand what is happening . . . we are in a time of rapid mutation."

Yes, the mutation through which we are passing is formidable. And the Church, which is *in* the world without being *of* the world, is undergoing the shock of it. Words, concepts, values are being renewed.

In our day and age science
and technology have revolu-
tionized our existence,
changing our way of living
and thinking and even changing certain ways we had
of representing to ourselves
the world, man and God
himself.

In an era of such essential
transformation, the Church,
desirous of assisting in the
resolution of contemporary
problems, has applied
the rules of modern language
and science to Revelation
in order that the truth of
God might be recognized as
the truth which can save
modern man.

What sounded true to previous generations sounds false today. This phenomenon is not recent. It had begun before the Council, and many Christians became estranged from the Church because they did not find in time solutions to the inevitable problems they were experiencing. The Council was conscious of coming late. It tried to see the situation clearly, very quickly, and remedy it.

THE EARTH IS NO LONGER THE CENTER OF OUR WORLD

Science has changed our vision of the world, and is doing so at an accelerating rate.

In biblical times the earth appeared to people as a flat surface overlapped by the vault of the sky. The relationship between God and men appeared a simple and familiar affair—God above, man below.

The man of the Middle Ages knew that the earth is round. The notions of above and below became relative, but the terrestrial globe remained the center of the universe.

At the Renaissance, with Copernicus and Galileo, it was certainly necessary to admit that the earth moved round the sun as one planet among others, and that it was not among the greatest of these planets. But the sun—the symbol of Christ—still appeared to be the center of the universe.

In 1918 Shepley discovered that the sun is not the center of our galaxy. The luminous and distant center of the stellar system in which we live is some thousands of light-years away. It manifests itself to us in the sky as the milky way, just as the lights of a large town are seen in the country thirty miles away as a lighter spot on the horizon. The sun is only a suburban star, at some distance from this central conglomeration.

And our galaxy in its turn is only one galaxy among others, one "universe" among others.

This "relativizes" us. What is man in these thousands of millions of worlds? He knows the most distant stars not as they exist today, but as they existed at the moment when they emitted the light which reaches us, that is to say thousands of millions of years ago. Many of these stars that we see are dead today, and our civilization can be known in these distant worlds only at the same interval of time, that is to say when humanity has disappeared with the extinction of the sun. So today we ask ourselves questions which make us dizzy. Are there a number of inhabited worlds? Are they inhabited by animals endowed with reason and with immortal souls? Are these also called to eternal life? Are they sinners? Are they redeemed?

WE ARE OLDER THAN WE USED TO THINK

Our representations of things become more deeply relative from the point of view of time. When I was a child some catechists still used to say—according to the biblical calculations accepted by Bossuet—that the world had begun 6,000 years before. In the eighteenth century Buffon did not dare to deviate too far from this figure because of censure. He dared only to multiply it by ten. He dated the origin of the world at some 60,000 years before, and it is in a manuscript correction on his own copy that he expressed his real conviction: 2,993,800 years. According to the hymns the time men had to wait for the coming of the Saviour was something like "4,000 years." This figure was liable to expansion. Before the war, so I have been told, a religious, a learned paleontologist, in difficulties about the censure of his order on the subject of the antiquity of man, had the following dialogue with his superior: "Father, I assure you that I cannot say less than 100,000 years."

"I allow you 50,000 of them," was the reply.

Today we have gone far beyond these difficulties: the number seems to be something like a million years, with the problem of a vanishing frontier. Where does man begin in the succession of anthropoids? At the same time, the number of human generations before Christ, before the revelation to Abraham, seems to be considerable. The creation of man, original sin, look different in this new setting. We are out of our element, bewildered, questioning. Was there only one couple of 'mutants' at the origin of the human race, or was there rather a whole group. In 1966 a commission nominated by the Pope studied these questions without finding in the new data provided by science any insurmountable doctrinal difficulty. But if doctrine remains the same, the perspective has changed, and theological formulations are in process of revision. Discussion of them is still in progress.

OUR HEART IS IN QUESTION

Must we not consider also the penetration of medical science into man's inmost physical being, the overwhelming change in the image we have of our own heart and its meaning? The "heart," in the spontaneous image we have of ourselves, and in the culture in which we have been brought up, has a symbolic value. This symbolism has been used and abused, by too material an interpretation, and a certain kind of picture and statue trade in the Sacred Heart has become intolerable to our contemporaries. The symbol has been blocked by the physical organ.

Following this line of thought certain nineteenth-century moralists were inclined to think that surgery on the heart could not be authorized: it was a sacred organ. Today we have grafts, human grafts it is true. The heart of a young woman who is dead may beat in the breast of a living man without making him aware of any inscrutable sensibility. The Cape surgeons envisage keeping human hearts in reserve by grafting them on to apes, and even one day grafting on to a man the heart of a beast. And the nearest, they say, would be the heart of a pig. What a convulsion in our vision of man, and our vision of sacred symbols!

What a question mark set against a certain statue and picture trade in the Sacred Heart!

To go deeper still, science has been studying unilaterally the conditioning of knowledge. Man used to have the simple conviction that he knew things as they are. Science reveals to him a different image of them, a surprising, inhuman image, reduced to figures. Indeed it devotes itself to such an extent to laying bare the conditioning of knowledge that we lose all sense of its meaning.

There is physical conditioning and biological conditioning: science has calculated that the different colors correspond to certain vibrations, characterized by their frequencies. It is the same with sounds. What we see, what we hear, seems to be reduced to a subjective resonance of this colorless and silent mechanical world. Intellectual activity is regarded as a function

of the brain. Knowledge which used to seem absolute has been relativized.

There is psycho-analytic conditioning: our images, our language, our conscious intentions appear to us today as the result of unconscious pressures whose real source escapes us. Our representations of things, even our religious representations, are subject to this criticism. We feel a need to "demythologize," or in other words to distinguish between what is essential in revelation and the "myths" or images of the past, through which men represented this to themselves.

Finally there is a sociological and historical conditioning. We know today to what degree social and cultural realities influence modes of knowledge which the ancients took at their face value. We have set up an imaginary museum of all cultures and all languages. Everything seems relative.

Let us beware of losing our balance under the impact of these discoveries. Science, to be sure, is doing useful work in identifying the material conditions of knowledge. But this conditioning is not knowledge itself. It is the means of knowledge. And by all these means— vibrations, nervous transmissions to the brain and so forth—human knowledge contacts reality. It contacts the other, in so far as it is other, the other to the knowing subject, according to this subject's own deep law which remains that of intentionality, the movement of the subject who knows towards the other which is known. The fact that colors are conditioned by vibrations does not abolish the world of colors. These are a means to a true knowledge of the world. We see them in the same way. Evolution has formed the eye to capture them. There are, and always have been, paintings which live in this world, and their importance in contemporary society only grows. All the conditions of knowledge are nothing but the under-side of knowledge, and knowledge itself retains all its spiritual value. One might be tempted to say that science shows us creation inside out. In the same way the makers of the Gobelin tapestries worked them on the wrong side, the side where they crossed and tied the threads. But

36

it was the right side which was made to be seen, and which is the reality itself of the work of art.

Nevertheless, man has undergone perhaps the deepest mutation he has ever known since his origin, at least the deepest for 12,000 years. Twelve thousand years ago, man the hunter and fisherman became man the tiller of the soil. He installed himself on the land to cultivate it. He made a calculation of genius, a long term calculation: the grain which dies in the ground can bring forth a hundredfold. It was within the framework of the agrarian civilization born of this calculation that the Gospel and its parables were preached.

But this agricultural world, this world of "culture" in every sense of the word, is tending to be replaced by another. Men are collecting into a mass. The towns which once used to contain only an infinite minority now include the majority. They tend to absorb 80 or 90 per cent of men in a world which is more and more remote from nature, while technology invades the countryside itself. Ways of life, ways of thought are being affected. The way in which the world, man and God himself present themselves to the mind is being changed.

At a depth beneath that of our representations of reality, it is culture itself which is being called in question in a world where the basic reference is no longer the act of cultivating, but the technological, mathematical, scientific act. So people sometimes talk about "deculturization," the end of "culture," the appearance of something else beyond culture. The triumph of technology is wonderful, but for the moment at least it is inhuman. It leaves us no peace. It tears from us our habitual ways and our tranquility. Every man who lives at all seriously the life of our time is continually changing his ways of thinking and acting, and is doing so more and more rapidly. He has to "regear" himself as we say every five years or even oftener. The man who lags behind in out-moded conceptions is counted out if only professionally. If he is at the head of some undertaking its affairs decline; if he is a technician he loses his job. In the same way, a faith which does not adapt itself to new conditions becomes attenuated.

DO NOT SACRIFICE THE SUBSTANCE FOR THE SHADOW

From this point of view the problem lies in adaptation. It is not easy, and the Christian can make two opposite sorts of mistake.

1. Some people throw themselves head-first into the adaptation movement. They abandon everything they have accepted the moment the least element in it seems to them to be falling into disuse. They have the illusion that we must begin all over again, start from scratch; they jettison the wisdom of experience and embark at their own risk on premature and superficial improvisations. Often they sacrifice the substance for the shadow, like the dog in the fable. They throw overboard the real values contained in the conceptual approximations of the last generation, and

replace them by non-values. In this way too many Christians are radically questioning Mary's virginity in aid of a naturalism foreign to the spirit of the Gospel, or again questioning original sin on behalf of an optimism which is given the lie by our hatreds and wars and crimes, and the secret poverty which every clear-headed man sees in the depths of his own heart.

The risk then is one of superficiality, of precipitation. Let us get it clear to ourselves that the mistake is not in going too fast, for we must go very fast today, but in starting wrong. An experienced skier can descend a slope at 60, 100 or 120 miles an hour, but someone who does not know how to keep his balance takes enormous risks in going ten times more slowly. He will not be able to stop himself, or turn aside to avoid the rock or precipice. People say he "goes beyond his means." In the same way an expert driver may do 200 or 300 miles an hour, but it can be madness for someone in L-plates to drive at 80, incapable as he is of reacting to the unexpected.

2. Other Christians make the opposite mistake. They refuse to adapt themselves. They act in a defensive, negative way against the difficulties which assail them on every side. They refuse to face facts or to see new problems. They make themselves a shell or put on armor. They maintain materially and without modification the formulas and representations of their faith. They do it no doubt with the best intentions, and in order to defend this precious treasure whose value they have reason to know. But often this rigidity

hardens them against their time, against other people and against themselves. They refuse to acknowledge undeniable values, and undeniable truths. Their human and Christian growth is arrested, like that of children who do not develop normally, and for this very reason become deformed. The obedience to God which inspires this second attitude has, to be sure, its value, but something is lacking. And Christians of this sort are unbalanced. Their light does not shine, and sometimes their witness is against the faith.

THE SYNOD'S CONCLUSIONS

The synod of bishops assembled in Rome in October 1967 grasped these problems. The first notion, which was the inspiration, as late as 1966, of Cardinal Ottaviani's inquiries about the "ten modern errors," was that it was a question as in the past of defining and condemning a certain number of heresies. The report read to the synod remained to a certain extent within this perspective.

The synod, gathered together in the Holy Spirit, felt the need to go beyond this method. It is not so much a matter today of specific errors which need to be fought, as of an overall effect of doubts and difficulties which need to be surmounted.

It seemed plainly evident then to the synod Fathers, illumined by the Holy Spirit, that it is not by anathemas that the God of love is revealed. The solutions of the problems before them called for positive and faithful research in the direction opened up by John XXIII, when he declared in the speech with which he opened the Council (*Enchiridion Vaticanum,* p. 45, n. 55):

"The deposit of faith, that is to say the truths contained in our doctrine, is one thing; the way they are expressed is another, provided the meaning and import are preserved."

A second thing seemed obvious in this connection: hard work and conscientious research are necessary. It is at this price that the faith will remain the same in a changing world. In an organism which is in process of growth, it is not enough that each organ should continue to remain as it is and fulfill its function; it has to be modified, each individual organ, in proportion to the change which is taking place in the body as a whole. To do the work involved the synod set up a commission of theologians chosen from the entire world. It will be their mission to solve the problems of our time, so that the revelation which God made to us once for all in the language of 2,000 years ago may be adjusted in its expression to the language and the discoveries of today. In short, the synod opened up scientific research in theology, so that the truth of God should remain truth, truth which will save the man of today, the man of space-travel and relativity.

But in this matter as in others research is not enough. While experts are working to find a long-term solution to the problems of hunger in the world, we must all eat every day; for man does not live on projects and research but on bread. In the same way, the ordinary believer cannot wait till the theologians have solved all the technical problems which are posed. His faith needs to be nourished and strengthened every day. It is like the situation in heart surgery. A man's circulation cannot be stopped while the operation is in progress. He would be dead. So the bishops at the synod were concerned for a second thing, that men should be given the daily bread of God's word, that research should not hold God and truth in suspense. Hence a double provision.

First they asked for a renewal in catechesis, so that God's message may be taught in a way adapted to children and to people today. This has been in operation since the Council. It was put in the hands of Cardinal Villot who had drawn the attention of the synod to the state of seminary studies.

The second project went further. It was decided

in October 1967, by the synod itself, that "a positive
pastoral declaration" should be worked out, which
would "help people today to see the problems of faith
in their context, as they present themselves to the mentality of modern men."

FAITH IS SIMPLE

One last remark needs to be added here, which
goes beyond the synod and brings us back to the Gospel itself. Faith is simple, and God has a secret pre-
dilection for the faith of the poor: "Blessed are the
poor, for theirs is the kingdom of heaven." Most
certainly it is necessary that theologians should do
their work, but it is not from their technical labors
that the best solution will come. It will come rather
from the life of Christian people, of those who live
the message of evangelical poverty. For they know
God better than scientists do, even if the scientists are
theologians.

St. Thomas, at the height of his theological science,
drew our attention to this. He said that an unlettered
woman of the people could know God better than he,
with all his discursive knowledge, thanks to the light
which the Lord gives to the poor: "I thank thee Father, Lord of heaven and earth, because thou hast
hidden these things from the wise and prudent, and
revealed them to babes" (Mt 11:25).

Yes, God is pleased to "bring to naught the wisdom of the wise" by that deeper wisdom with which
he inspires the humble. It is from that wisdom that what

is essential to the regeneration of faith will come.

Twenty centuries of the Church's experience prove to us that this idea is not a myth. The "poor woman," the woman without culture who is wiser than St. Thomas Aquinas and all the theologians together, God knows countless instances of her exist, and that theologians often owe to her the best of what they make explicit in their work. They received from their mother their first perception of the living God. From this multitude of unknown women, there is one who emerges, well-known for her humility itself, the Virgin Mary, who, through her consent to the Word of God, formed Christ himself.

The Blessed Virgin is the "model" of this faith which God gives to the simple and poor. That is the secret which we shall try to explore in the next chapter: faith is a certainty. It is stronger than all the difficulties of yesterday and today. For this certainty is not according to the measure of this world's knowledge and understanding but according to the measure of God who gives it.

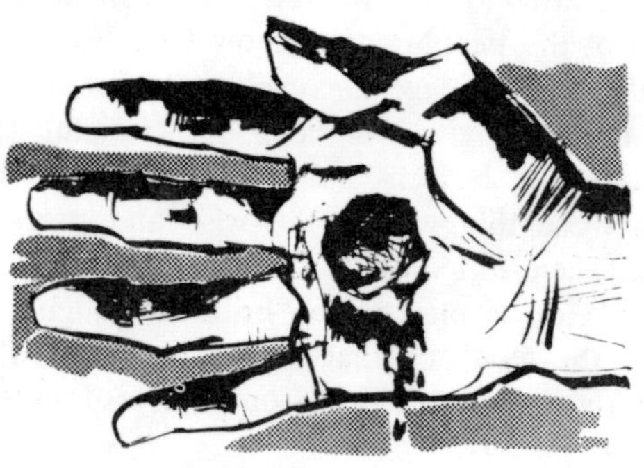

Is Faith A Certainty?

III   IS FAITH A CERTAINTY?

What is faith? That is the real question. Perhaps we rushed into print too soon. Perhaps we have arrived too late at "the crisis of faith." It was necessary to put it into its context, but what matters is not the crisis but the faith.

Scripture itself gives us a definition: "Faith is the substance of things hoped for, the conviction of realities not seen (Heb 11:1).

This is a definition by the very object of faith: not a remote abstraction, an idea in itself, but a life which God offers us. God reveals himself to us as our salvation, present and eternal; for we need to be saved from evil both here and now and in the life to come.

A FOLLY

This salvation, revealed in and by Jesus Christ, is not obvious to the senses. That is why St. Paul speaks of "the conviction of realities not seen." In the first epistle to the Corinthians (1: 19-31), he goes further. Not only is what faith reveals invisible, but it is "a stumbling-block to Jews and a folly to pagans."

It is a stumbling-block to Jews that the transcendent God should become man, of the race of men, that he should die for us in this human life which he has personally taken upon himself for us.

It is a folly to pagans that one should believe in the resurrection of the body, in eternal life, in the Gospel and the strange blessedness which it offers:

> "Blessed are the poor. . . Blessed are those who mourn. . . Blessed are those who suffer persecution". . . .

The world says the opposite:

> "Blessed are the rich, blessed are those who laugh, blessed are those on whom we heap praise and honor."

But the Gospel insists:

> "Woe to you who are rich. . . Woe to you that laugh now. . . Woe to you when all men speak well of you; for so their fathers did to the false prophets."

Must we say then that faith is only a gamble, that it is a bet? Must we say, *"Credo quia absurdum* (I believe because it is absurd), and the more absurd it is, the more faith is really faith?" To all these questions the answer is no.

Faith is not a gamble. It is what is surest in a man's life. It is a more than human certainty, based on the Word of God, who is Truth himself.

A DARK AND LUMINOUS CLOUD

Faith is a light, but not a light like other lights.

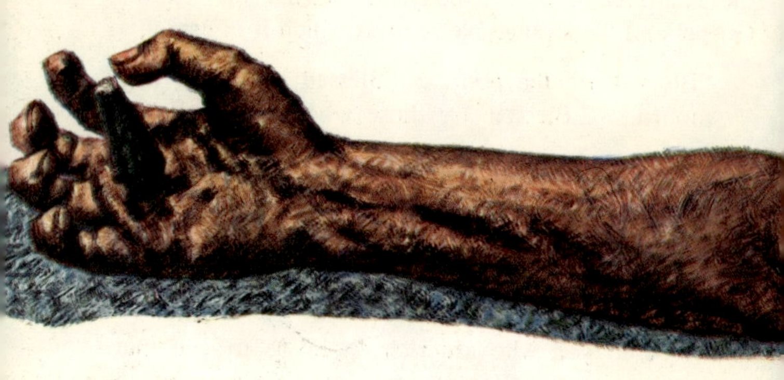

What is faith? The Bible
presents it as the foundation
of our hope and the con-
viction of that which we do
not see. Faith is not a
gamble. It is the surest thing
in the life of man. It is
superhuman certainty rooted
in God himself.

Those who believe in the depth of their heart understand that well enough before anyone explains it to them. The faith which lights their path is like the cloud which guided the Jews in the desert, dark in daylight, shining at night, because it tempers for us the light of God. Those who expect from faith a light too bright and palpable are disappointed; those who go out into the dark discover for themselves the light of faith.

It might be compared to the star which guides the navigator: it does not light up the waves through which the ship travels in darkness, but it gives him a sure direction.

As faith is a light but not like other lights, so it is a certainty but not like other certainties. It is not like the certainty which one has when one touches something palpably, not like that which Thomas the apostle demanded:

"Unless I place my finger in the mark of the nails, and place my hand in his side, I will not believe" (Jn 20:25).

"Blessed are those who have not seen, and yet believe," Jesus said to him.

Nor is faith the certainty of mathematical reasoning, which imposes its conclusions on its own internal evidence.

The certainty of faith is not measured by the verifiable lucidity of its conclusions, although faith has its light; it is not measured by the weightiness of its reasons, although faith has very weighty reasons. Nor is it measured by the strength of the will which adheres to it, even though faith does demand a firm adherence of the will.

The certainty of faith obtains not from a humanly verifiable evidence, but from the simple value of God's witness. If we believe, it is because God has revealed it. There are people we believe simply because we take their word for what they say, although it does not appear evident to us and even surprises us. We credit them because they are creditable witnesses. We who are not scientists believe many things because men of science say they can prove them. We simply take their word for it. And in the same way we believe those who talk to us about what they have seen and we have not seen. Most of the things we know, we know not by experience but by report, because we have confidence in those who understand them and talk to us about them. And we base on this solid certainties.

The most solid certainty we could have would be one which came to us from God, the supreme witness, the absolute Truth, God who alone can talk about God, *knowing* what he is talking about.

That is the essence of faith: adherence to God who reveals and is revealed, to God who unveils himself to us or rather who unveils to us that life in himself which he offers to us. "God is Love . . . and we have believed in Love," St. John sums it up (1 Jn 4:8 and 16).

The particular truths detailed in dogmas and doctrines are only facets of this truth: the love of God,

God who *is* love, given to us, shared with us through Christ.

Faith is God's gift at two levels. In the first place he has revealed himself objectively, once for all, in Jesus Christ. Then he manifests the truth of his revelation in the heart of each generation of Christians, in the heart of each individual Christian in the Church. Faith is, for each of us personally, a gift from God.

HOW GOD SPEAKS TO EACH OF US

It is not that God repeats literally to each Christian the words of revelation. What was said once by Christ

has been said once for all. The Church transmits it faithfully and in the objective sense. But the inner gift of God in the heart of everyone who believes illumines the words which were revealed once for all. It manifests that t h e s e words which are "folly" in the eyes of men are the wisdom of God. God lights up for us the reasons for faith. Without his light these reasons

52

would be like certain manuscripts, indecipherable. The ink of these manuscripts melts into the color of the parchment, and one needs to apply a chemical to reveal the effaced handwriting. It is that sort of thing that the Holy Spirit does for us. Through him the letter of the Gospel becomes light and life. So we can pass by a scriptural text many times without grasping the meaning of it, and then, at last, one day it becomes luminous and arresting. This light thrown upon it comes from the Holy Spirit. It is the witness of God in us. This interior and secret action creates a certainty stronger than any other, superior to every ordeal, as is manifested by the witness of the martyrs. God communicates to us his own certainty.

This light God imposes on no one, but refuses to no one. A man may accept it or refuse it. But there is no faith without the gift of this light, the star which guides our journey through the night.

It is necessary to insist on this, for it is not just a gratuitous opinion; it is the teaching of scripture. St. John puts it very explicitly in his first epistle: "He who believes in the Son of God has the testimony in himself" (1 Jn 5:10). And inversely: "He who does not believe God, has made him a liar, because he has not believed the testimony that God has borne to his Son" (5:11).

This witness he calls an interior *unction* of the Holy Spirit, from whom all our knowledge comes:

"But you have an unction from the Holy One and you all know" (2:20). And again: "As for you, the unction which you have received from him abides

in you, and you have no need that anyone should
teach you" (2:26).

This does not mean that the interior witness of God
makes the teaching of the Church unnecessary; on the
contrary the function of this interior witness is to give
light and life to the exterior teaching, which in this
way acquires the force of inner evidence received di-
rectly from God. God gives this gift normally in and
through the Church. Where the Church is, there the
Spirit is.

It is this inner evidence which Christ teaches also
in St. Matthew's Gospel (11:25): "I thank thee
Father . . . because thou hast hidden these things from
the wise and prudent and revealed them to babes.
For so Father it seemed good in thy sight." It is a
matter here still of the revelation given objectively to
all in the same way, for the Gospel preached is the
same for all; but God illumines the message in the
heart of the humble and the poor, while his word remains hidden, as if in a foreign language, from those
who are closed to the witness of the Spirit.

One could multiply the references: "No one can
come to me, unless my Father draw him" (Jn 6:45),
and "the Holy Spirit whom the Father will send in
my name will teach you all things, and bring to your
remembrance all that I have said to you" (24:26).
In other words the Holy Spirit in the Church recalls
and gives life to what Christ taught in his own person
through his life and his words.

"I have yet many things to say to you but you

cannot bear them now. When he, the Spirit of truth comes, he will guide you into all truth, for he will not speak on his own authority, but whatever he hears he will speak, and he will declare to you the things to come" (16:12-13). These verses indicate the unobtrusive way in which the Spirit witnesses in men's hearts. He does not add to Christ's teaching or say anything different from it, nor does he even repeat it; but he illumines what was said once for all. So at Pentecost the apostles grasped the meaning of sayings that they had not understood before.

One might read on this subject other texts of scripture; for instance 1 Corinthians 2: 19-21; and 4:6; Hebrews 8: 10-12 and Jeremiah 31: 33-34.

There is here a constant and solid teaching, and authentic Christian experience verifies its truth. In the measure that we really live the faith, we know it; we know that it is a something we receive, a gratuitous gift; we know that it is a more than human light. And yet the act of faith is a free and personal act. And it is in a commitment, that of a conversion or that of responding to a vocation, for example, that the light is given.

HOW ARE WE TO OVERCOME 'TEMPTATIONS AGAINST FAITH'?

Anyone who has understood the real nature of faith, its foundation in God himself and its certainty based on him, will avoid many false steps in difficulties or temptations against faith, as the experienced mountaineer avoids the wrong reflex, which precipitates a fall in clutching at security.

What, basically, is a temptation against faith? It is often a sudden concrete awareness of what St. Paul meant by saying that faith is a "stumbling-block" and a "folly." We lose our balance when we happen to " "realize," in the context of some concrete occasion or by pure grace, the stark meaning of the ready-made formulas to which we have become accustomed, which we have learnt by heart: "God is made man" for instance. When the word *God* suddenly takes on for us its whole meaning, this statement seems incredible. Indeed it is incredible, humanly speaking, that the transcendent Creator by whose will all things remain in being should have taken upon himself the limited existence of a creature. And if we realize that this same God died on the Cross at the end of his human adventure, the "stumbling-block" rears itself up like a mountain. If we realize that he intends to give us himself as food, that the host made of flour and in no way changed as far as we can see physically, is his body,

56

then, like those to whom he spoke in Galilee, we think, "This is a hard saying. Who can hear it?" (Jn 6:60).

And yet what is beyond us is grace. We know how the words which have suddenly taken on their meaning outstrip our minds, how God's gift is beyond anything we can conceive or imagine, and we are disturbed as Moses was disturbed in the presence of the burning bush, or St. Peter when he said, "Depart from me, for I am a sinful man, O Lord." The temptation of our humanity then is to refuse the divine measure, to fall back on the human measure, to reject as absurd the disproportionate truth which has suddenly invaded us.

When we are suddenly seized like this with the vertigo of doubt, in the face of the disturbing wisdom of God, and we try to defend our faith, the first reflex is to argue about the matter discursively, to try and reason it out, to look for proofs. But in this sort of situation proofs vanish, our reasoning powers refuse to function. This is due simply to the fact that the doubt we are entertaining withdraws us from the witness of God in us. In looking for our certainty outside him we can only entangle ourselves more in our doubt—like the driver stuck in the snow who accelerates madly, makes his wheels run round and round on the same spot, and so digs himself further in, so that he will never free himself if he is obstinately bent on doing so. Or, to take an even better analogy, we are like a man caught in quicksand. Our attempts to reason involve us more deeply in doubt, like the attempts to extricate themselves of those lost in the dangerous zones in the bay of Mont-Saint-Michel. The movements which they multiply to get out, plunge them further in, and it cannot be otherwise.

Another reflex is to cling to belief by an act of will, to chase away the difficulty or objection. This can be a provisional means of defence. But it is not a solution. It is an attitude too like the reflexes of the obstinate person who wants to know nothing but his own ideas. The abuse of their will leads some Christians into narrow, sectarian attitudes, which do not make for a healthy and open and radiant faith.

OUR CERTAINTY COMES FROM GOD

What we must be fully conscious of in these difficult situations is that faith is of its nature dark, like a night studded with stars. The stars make us certain of our direction, but they do not illumine the ground on which we are walking.

58

 What we must specially be aware of is that faith is *given*. Its certainty comes from God who witnesses to it, and not from any reasons which would allow us to argue to God from outside. This would be as hopeless an undertaking as building the tower of Babel to reach the sky. For anyone who has understood the nature of faith as we find it in the scriptures, the basic attitude to take up when attacked by doubt is to put oneself in the hands of him from whom faith comes, in the hands of him who is the source of certainty, to pray to him in the darkness. He is there, ready to answer sooner or later. It is in this way that faith is able to recontact its real origin, the God of love who reveals himself and is his own witness.

Then, little by little, the "objection" will itself begin to shine; the "folly" will reveal another sort of wisdom—"Yes, Lord, you love us as much as this. You, through whom everything exists and without whom nothing exists, became this little child for us, this criminal condemned to death, this food. Such is the folly of your love: 'Lord, I believe; but help my unbelief.' "

It is in this personal adherence to God that the peace which remains below the surface, deep in our being, will reach again the level of our conscious life. It will become green again, like the broken branch which is bound to the trunk so that it may draw from the trunk its healing sap.

The difficulties and objections can then be (and indeed must be) looked at again, examined, seen in their context, overcome. This may take years of hard work, generations in the life of the Church, and it can be extremely exacting. That does not matter much if the essential that nothing can take from us remains; for God is there, even in the darkest tunnels.

So this is the certainty of faith. It rests not on merely human foundations but on God himself, and *ipso facto* therefore it goes beyond our human powers. This is its paradox, that it is the most powerful of all certainties, since it resides in God, but at the same time it is dark, vulnerable, difficult. It can be attacked by all sorts of oppositions and contradictions, inner and outer, but, as Newman said, "a thousand difficulties do not make one doubt."

A LIFE

Faith is like life itself, at once weak and strong, at once fragile and unconquerable. Let us remember

the grain of wheat sown in the ground, which seems
to die when it is in fact living a new life. . . . Let us
remember the plants which survive by clinging to the
almost non-existent scrap of soil in the crevice of
a wall or a rock. Faith too is a life; it needs nurture;
it needs to be cultivated. That is what we must think
about now.

Living the Truth

Our knowledge is dead if it is not accompanied by action. As a matter of fact, it approaches a kind of ignorance. In true faith, knowledge and action are inseparable from one another.

IV LIVING THE TRUTH

How are we to cultivate faith? How are we to strengthen it, to nourish it, to make it reveal itself?

We have, of course, to see that it is an instructed faith, to bring it into the daylight, to keep in contact with the Gospel itself and read generally to nourish our faith. This is obvious and we all know it, and this is not the place to insist on it.

The Gospel according to St. John gives us a rule which is less well-known, more secret, one of the sayings of Christ: "He who does the truth comes to the light."

It is a stark saying, and translations, not daring to reproduce it literally, try to soften it: "He who lives by the truth"... "He who puts the truth into practice"....

The Gospel is very modern in the sense that it has not a passive conception of knowledge and love. The "truth revealed" is not a truth of abstract theories which one knows first and applies afterwards. In a faith which is real everything is inseparable: if action proceeds from knowledge, knowledge is fulfilled in action.

St. Thomas Aquinas, who is held to be the greatest "speculative" theologian of all time, understood this well enough. He sets it down at the very beginning of the *Summa*: theology is not a purely speculative science, it is a "practical science." One really knows God only in living. . . .

It is so in all kinds of knowledge. Music, for instance, calls in differing degrees for involvment, active participation; without it sounds would remain indistinguishable. The man who has no ear for music cannot tell a masterpiece from a cacophany.

The knowledge of faith is a *"praxis"*; that is to say a knowledge which constructs man and is perfected in this construction itself. It is not like Marxism a praxis of struggle, but a praxis of love, of meeting, of communication.

"My little children, let us not love in word or in tongue, but in deed and in truth" (Jn 3:18). And again, "And by this we know that we know him, if we keep his commandments. He who says, 'I know him,' and does not keep his commandments is a liar, and the truth is not in him. . . . He who says he is in the light and hates his brother is still in darkness" (2:3).

It is so in all knowledge of a personal order, all knowledge which is bound up with love. Friendship is a construction; love is a construction. The impossible love of Tristan and Yseult is only a hope of love, or a despair of love. The myth is tied to a pessimistic conception, according to which love is a mirage, and its realization is disillusionment. Perfect love, ideal love, can be only unreal love. But what is this love which sees without meeting, which meets without conceiving, or which conceives without giving birth? Is not this love itself an illusion?

Authentically human love has to be sought among men and women who have known how to take on themselves, together and for always, the better and the worse, the joys and the sorrows, the trials and the labors of life. Right up to the end of their days, they look on all they have realized, both in themselves and outside themselves, and specially on their children, without regret and without nostalgia. Their love is made of all the threads they have woven in the woof and weft of time, of all that they have constructed together. Without all this it would not be the same love. It comes from their conjugal faith; for marriage also begins in faith, in the solemn promise through which bride and groom trust and commit, bind and affiance themselves to each other, in good faith and complete confidence.

The analogy of faith in God with what St. Augustine called the "faith of marriage" is revealing. Marriage also is a love which proceeds from knowledge. But this knowledge is not of a scientific sort. The way the doctor or the psychiatrist knows Mary or John is not the way they know each other, in their "interpersonal relationship" as we say today. Their knowledge implies commitment, a reciprocal gift of themselves. It is perfected in this exchange, in their common life together. It fashions a new reality, a common personality which is no longer that of either, but of the two together, in their identity, their complementarity, their communion.

This knowledge ordinarily develops from fantasy to truth, from illusion to authenticity, without which there would of necessity be disillusionment. It is characteristic of a successful marriage that it has no nostalgia for the time when husband and wife were simply engaged, as if it were regretting a vanished happiness; it lives in the present, turned towards the future, the future of children and grand-children.

At its transcendental level, faith in Jesus Christ is also knowledge of a person, of the person of the incarnate Word. It is bound up with a common life, with a common labor together, with the formation of a new being, the mystical body of Christ. It is perfected in this co-operation in the work of salvation. It is in becoming involved in this work, in "doing this truth" that one "comes to the light."

In many Christians the excessive obscurity of their faith, its distant and hazy character, leads to a faith without works, without commitment, a disembodied faith. It never takes flesh. It never "comes to the light." Many Christians have absorbed, from the catechism or elsewhere, certain "truths," too abstractly inculcated. On occasion they are fond of reasoning about them, giving a dissertation—notably in the presence of a priest—with the secret hope of proving by their verbal activity that a certain faith still exists in them. But their life, their pursuits, their interests, their calling, their desires are built on quite other bases. That is why their faith declines. They regret it. They hope that sometime they will be able to snap out of the situation, but they do not know how.

The way of salvation is traced out in the Gospel, in the Sermon on the Mount. Those who love the poor and know how to give themselves for them: those who visit prisoners, feed the hungry, clothe the naked, care for the sick, work for the realization of peace, these will come to the light.

But though it is traced out, the path remains a secret one. Each person, each generation has to rediscover it, to clear the way along it, according to the vocation given. Our own time has a great deal to do in this regard. The Church is still too much a spectacle, an alibi, not enough a reality to which we are committed and in which we are involved. Many are content to accept as their own whatever the Pope does. "As for what I believe, go and ask Rome," answered a well-known Christian to an inquiry about his faith. "As for what I am doing for the Kingdom of God" some others might answer, "go and ask Rome. I accept everything that is being done there." But in this way the Church does not exist in its foundations, in the particular churches all over the world. What is believed and done in Rome is of little import if it is not effectively believed and shared by each individual Catholic. In the same way what is eaten in Rome cannot nourish those who are hungry on the other side of the world. Truth is a food which no one can eat for anyone else.

To realize the saying of the Gospel, "Blessed are the peacemakers, it is not enough to follow the Pope's activities in the service of peace—his speeches, his contacts, his diplomacy—however admirable these

may be; nor is it enough to applaud them. What is necessary is that each Christian should be in his own context an agent of peace, both local and universal, both in his own social relationships and in forming public opinion.

It is not enough to follow the meetings of the Pope and the Patriarch Athenagoras; what is necessary is that at the grass roots level small groups of Christian people everywhere should establish ecumenical contacts of the same sort, as the Council suggested.

It is not enough to give to charitable organizations "in the places where the poor are"; what is necessary is that Christian people acting as a leaven everywhere should shoulder their personal responsibilities in the world. And so on with all the demands of the Gospel.

The ways of giving ourselves, which allow us to "do the truth" as Christ invites us, are many. We may give ourselves liturgically, in really active participation in the prayer of the Church. Where liturgical reform is properly understood, properly realized, properly lived, it brings about *ipso facto* concrete re-orientations in ordinary life. For the distinguishing characteristic of Christian liturgy is that it is not an end in itself. It is done so that it may be prolonged by the oblation of the whole of life—what St. Paul called "sacrifices of praise." He meant by that the very tissue of our life and death, lived and suffered according to the Gospel, impregnated with love, given to God and men. This sacrifice no one can offer for us. It is irreplaceable in the mystical body. John XXIII well knew how to offer the sacrifice of his geniality, his smile, his continuous welcome, and above all of his death agony. Do you remember how many times he came out of his coma at the end, in order to give himself to God in prayer for men, with highly concrete intentions connected with the Church's needs at the time, in

Greece and elsewhere? This sacrifice which he celebrated we are called to celebrate also in our own way. For he offered it not in virtue of his papal or episcopal status, but in virtue of that "common priesthood" which belongs to all the faithful, according to the doctrine of the Council.

TRUTH IS LIVED IN COMMON

And finally there is a golden rule which can be a great help in "doing the truth." God communicates himself to men who are bound together in a human communion, a human fellowship. In the Old Testament he chose a people, a nation, and it was there that he revealed himself, that he laid the foundations of our faith. Then Jesus formed "the twelve" together, in a rigorously common life. And it is in the Church which he entrusted to them that he continues to give himself. However important the universal Church may be, this communion is realized practically only on a human scale. The early Christians lived in small communities centered in the houses where the Eucharist was celebrated, for there were not yet churches. These communities swarmed as often as there was no longer room for everyone in the house. Then other houses became centers where the common life was received and from which it was radiated. Such were the "primitive churches." The word church means assembly.

I have seen a renaissance of this pattern of grouping in Latin America, especially in Mexico. At Cuernavaca

for instance, in 1967, a priest was sent into a quarter little touched by the local parishes. One of the Christians there gave him a welcome and took charge of him. One of the two rooms of the house became the place where Mass was celebrated. The room soon became too small. The man destroyed the wall which divided his house in two in order to be able to welcome everybody. The dynamism of early Christianity was lived again in concrete terms in this suburb.

It is this need of a common life which explains the birth and multiplication of religious orders. In the Middle Ages the Church was disturbed about the number of them, and councils intervened with increasing severity to forbid the founding of new ones. But the number has only grown with time, and this is partly due to the fact that there do not exist outside them, living and demanding communities of the style of the early centuries of the Church. We have here something which is imperative for the Gospel, a lesson from history and experience: *Christ is discovered in community,* and the individualistic faith withers.

This law has its foundation in the doctrine of the mystical body itself. We are redeemed not in a state of isolation, but through our incorporation into Christ, the incorporation realized in baptism, and strengthened by the other sacraments.

But it is not enough that the sacraments should be administered in material terms. What is necessary is that the body should live as a body, and therefore that a human fellowship should be realized, where the stronger carry the weaker and find themselves strengthened by this responsibility. In other words, the mystical body must not be an abstraction, but a living reality. And for that, there is need of communities where contact and reciprocal communication are effective.

That is why I have often given this advice to young people who have come to me at the end of their catechism classes, or on leaving a Catholic school.

If you want to keep your faith, find a living Christian group of some sort, whose life you can share. Look for it at your own level, according to your own possibilities. If you find it, the rest will come.

Sometimes I have added, when it was in the confessional, "I won't give you any other penance."

These groups with a common life on a human scale are indispensable in order that the mystical body should become an experienced reality. Certainly it must not be a matter of closed, exclusive groups, but of groups which welcome new members and open out on to larger groups. Groups of this kind have become for Christians today, in our tentacular civilization, a necessary means to prevent the institutional Church from becoming a distant abstraction, as it is for too many Catholics.

Groups of this kind can be very different: they may be based on one's locality, or the house where one lives, or one's professional life; they may be ecumenical or liturgical groups, or associations for helping the poor or giving aid to underdeveloped countries. It is important that the group should find its own form of common prayer, in which it can express itself authentically, and be authentically united in God. Indeed it is by means of a living liturgy that present day risks of secularization are averted. So Christian action in service of the world will not be enclosed within the secular limits of this world, but will find its authentic source in the mystical reality of Christ. Horizontal action in the world of men will find its vertical inspiration and end in God.

How to multiply these open communities where the mystical body may be effectively lived in an effective communion, and restructure in this way from below the too large communities of the parish and the Church as a whole, is certainly one of the key problems for the future of belief, one of the relevant investigations actually being made at the present time.

A Crisis of Growth

Science today takes care
of a lot of little jobs that
up to now were attributed,
almost irreverently, to God.
Herein lies much of the
problem of faith. This is
unfortunate for it should
rather lead us to a deepening
of our concept of God
whose presence in the world
is much more universal
and profound than we ever
before realized. God is not
solitude personified but
the perfection of Love.
In him are all things. His is
the fulness of Presence
which is realized so ineffably
in the Eucharist.

V A CRISIS OF GROWTH

Certain people are led to see in the present "crisis" of faith a mortal crisis. Some of these people are pessimistic and anxious Christians; others are enemies of Christianity, who rejoice at the prospect. The diagnosis they have in common is based on the importance of the changes which are affecting the Church today, and on the uncertainty which has seized her in the face of certain problems. They are impressed too by the contrast between this humility on the part of the Church and the triumphs of human progress, in space travel, in medicine, and elsewhere. God seems to have become unnecessary. Have not science and technology triumphed precisely in so far as they have sought solutions to problems on a material plane, without resorting to divine causality?

So long as the rainbow was regarded as a gratuitous act of God, nothing was understood about this phenomenon. It was explained when it could be regarded as a case of refraction, according to prismatic laws. In the same way, as long as certain diseases were regarded merely as a consequence of sin the remedies we are all talking about today were not sought. These were found when the cause of these diseases was looked for on the physical plane, in relation to microbes and anatomical and physiological processes.

God conceived as a *Deus ex machina,* as a watch-maker who had regulated his watch badly and was always intervening to put it right, is repugnant to our epoch, and scarcely encourages a respect for transcendence. It is not in this fashion that God is Creator. His presence in the world is more universal and more profound. What is called in question by science is not the real God, but a collection of paltry roles which we have insultingly asked him to play. The progress of science invites us to see God in a more honorable light, and, at the same time, to see man himself in a more honorable light, whom God, according to Genesis (1:28), set to reign over creation: "Fill the earth and subdue it; and have dominion over the fish of the sea and over the birds of the air, and over every living thing that moves upon the earth."

Human progress realizes this dominion, in discovering the strictness of the created order. God no longer appears as a being hidden in the gaps and insufficiencies of the world, but more deeply, as Being not of the world, anterior to the world, through whom all that is subsists. We grasp better that he is the "wholly Other," that his being is at a different level from the being of the world. He is not a cause like other causes, but the first cause, without interfering with the secondary causes which operate rigorously within the order of creation. Certainly Almighty God *can* interfere, intervene in the order which he has established. That is what is called a "miracle," but it is clearer to us today that the wisdom of God does not multiply miracles, and realizes them unobtrusively without turn-ing nature upside down, rather using nature in an exceptional way, as we see in the cures brought about at Lourdes.

When Gargam was cured there, he began to walk suddenly, after long months confined to his bed. He weighed at the time 88 lbs., half his normal weight, and it was the working of his own physical organism which reconstituted the flesh and the muscles. In the same way, when a deep wound or sore is healed at Lourdes, the gaping hole is not filled in by a creative act: there are rapid healing mechanisms which recon-stitute the tissues, and a scar remains. God's presence in the world is much more radical than these rare and unobtrusive interventions. It lies in the very existence of the world, which remains in being through his creative will, through his "Word" as scripture says.

In the same way again, God did not save the world by magic or by a demonstration of his almighty power, but by coming and entering into it, humbly, in poverty, without *éclat,* according to a natural process whose miraculous element remains a mystery we cannot grasp. The virginal conception remained during their lifetime the secret of Joseph and Mary. Christ was formed slowly in her, in the course of nine months, as every other child is. He grew up in the poor village of Naz-areth. And it was in this human powerlessness, taken upon himself for our sake, that he manifested his deepest nature. He is Love even more than Power.

It was so, that he wished, above all, to be inte-grated into the human family, to be with men and

among them in order to give himself to them.

It was so, that he revealed that God is not solitude but the perfection of love: that is, the perfection of unity in plurality, the perfection of identity in communication, the perfection of those who look at each other and are one. He revealed himself as the Son of the Father, and manifested the Spirit which is the very bond of their love.

It was so, too, that he manifested to men that what is best in them, what is best in creation, is also love, created in the image of God. One can understand then the place he gave love in creation, and why he multiplied there the various reflections of transcendent love.

So he expressed strength and aspiration in the love of fathers for their sons, and in the love of children for their father gratitude and admiration; in the love of mothers, tenderness; in friendship, the light of understanding.

And it is realities such as these that are the real means of salvation, not magic prodigies, but the love of God bearing fruit in the hearts of men.

PRAYER THAT IS ALWAYS ANSWERED

To understand God in this way is not to diminish him. On the contrary it is to recognize more surely his real nature, his real greatness, so different from the inflated notions of greatness that man in his sin pursues. Looking at God from this point of view invites us to look for him at his own level and not elsewhere; it invites us to ask him for what he intends to give us for our own good, in the way he has arranged, and not for a thousand other things such as spoiled children might ask from their blinded fathers.

People are sometimes shocked that certain prayers are not "answered," when Christ said, "Whatever you ask the Father in my name he will give it to you." But what they do not notice enough is the condition, "in my name." One cannot ask just anything at all of the Father in the name of Christ. One can ask only what is in accord with the Christ of the Gospel. That one will be given, infallibly, if one asks it with faith and love and perseverance, in order to exercise the responsibilities one has been given by God. But to ask that the rest should be "heard," would be to abase at the same time both God and man.

One could go through all doctrines or aspects of doctrine like this, and one would see that the famous "crisis of faith" about which we talk derives above all from the necessity of sloughing off naïve ways of representing the faith, ways which are often unworthy both of God and of man, so that we may grasp better the essentials which have been neglected.

A EUCHARISTIC CRISIS OR A EUCHARISTIC RENEWAL?

Take for instance the Eucharist. It is sometimes said that there have been diminutions here. It is true that there have been some diminutions: Benediction and perpetual adoration are rarer than they used to be. Isn't it faith in the real Presence which is in question? Some people ask themselves this, and even go so far as to suspect this or that priest of no longer believing in it. What exactly is happening in this sphere on the scale of the Church, on the scale of history?

After Bérenger had questioned the real Presence

in the Middle Ages, and especially after the Protestant crisis, Catholicism, in reaction, put the whole emphasis on it. It was the central point in preaching about the Eucharist, and religious practice developed in this direction for three hundred years. Different kinds of adoration multiplied—annual, monthly, weekly, daily, perpetual—and religious orders or associations put in charge of mounting a guard before the monstrance also multiplied. But other aspects of Eucharistic doctrine were neglected, not always without deviations as a result.

It was strange enough for instance to have Benediction immediately after a high Mass as if that could add anything to it. The liturgical renewal set in motion by the Council involves more discerning customs in this matter, which are spreading very quickly among sensitive communities, the custom for instance of leaving a time for adoration *during the Mass itself,* before Communion and, for a longer time, after Communion. After Communion the habit is spreading of making a common thanksgiving in silence sitting down to adore together the Christ who has come into the hearts of all and each, receiving in spirit the spiritual food— which is more important than looking at the appearance under which it is given.

SEEKING THE REALITY IN ITS FULLNESS

This development of Eucharistic faith and practice is not a diminution, but a deepening and widening.

88

It is the pursuit of the whole reality, setting a value not on the mere fact of the Presence, but on the totality of the gift involved in the Eucharist, in its meaning and in its fruits.

The Mass is not just a material accomplishing of a presence of Christ. It perpetuates the whole mystery of Christ, the sacrifice in which he involved himself to the death. He who is both man and God is given to us there, not statically but dynamically. The saving sacrifice of the Cross is actualized, made present, as well as the Resurrection and the consummation in heaven. And all this in order that we may share in it. In the Mass Christ gives himself to his Church so that each individual Christian may be fed: "Take and eat." In France and elsewhere the time when manifestations of the real Presence multiplied was also the time when people went rarely to Communion, and when they often did so outside the Mass, outside the natural context, so that the meaning and effect were diminished.

Today, the communal value of the Eucharist is better understood. We have discovered again that it is the sacrament of charity. It binds closely together those who eat together. It involves them in loving one another as Christ has loved them. This is a demand inscribed in the very sign of the broken and shared bread, and the wine drunk from the same cup, the sign that the Council wished to put back into the light of its full significance, by authorizing the Communion of the faithful from the chalice.

The meaning of this symbol and the involvement it implies was brought home to me very deeply one day by my father, who was an architect, and was simply telling me how he used to perform one of his professional duties. He was sometimes designated as an expert by the court whose mission it is in a law-suit to bring about an "agreement between the parties if such can be made," according to the juridical formula. As a Christian he very much liked this duty of conciliation. He used to study the problem carefully in its context, receive the arguments of each side separately, and look for an equitable solution for the benefit of everybody. When he had found it, he used to try to get it accepted, first by one side and then by the other. When the agreement between them seemed to him to be ripe, he drew up the terms ready for signature, and at last brought the contesting parties together. But before proposing that they should sign, he put on the table a bottle of wine. He filled the glasses and took his own in his hand ready to touch it to theirs. "When people have drunk together they always sign."

"But then," I asked, "is your reconciliation infallible?"

"No," he said, "for in some cases one or the other hesitates. Sometimes he will go as far as taking the glass in his hand, but when the time comes to touch it, he puts it back on the table saying, 'No, I won't drink.' Then the thing is a failure. There will be long court proceedings. But in our part of the country when two men have drunk together, reconciliation is already made: they always sign."

Do Christians perceive this demand for friendship between those who have drunk together? Do they grasp how much deeper is its necessity between those who share the body and blood of Christ? If too many Christians remain the slaves of their own spites and grudges is it not because the liturgical rite itself has not made this demand—to which every decent person is sensitive—obvious enough? We are making some progress today in this direction.

We are, too, rediscovering the more remote bearing of the Eucharist, its bearing upon the future, what the theologians call its "eschatological dimension"— in other words the meaning of St. Paul's words, "as often as you eat this bread and drink this cup you proclaim the Lord's death until he comes" (1 Cor 11:26).

The real Presence is thus put back into its whole context, not diminished but enriched, less "material," more abundant in its consequences. In concentrating on the presence some people came to isolate it from everything else, to stifle its own dynamism, to reduce it. They fell too easily into representing the Eucharist as an *inclusion* of Christ *in* the consecrated bread and wine. People used to talk about "the prisoner in the tabernacle." These are false expressions. Christ is not a *prisoner,* he who gives himself in the wonder of his universal communication to all times and all places. He is wholly in all of them, wholly in each person, through this mysterious presence able to be indefinitely multiplied according to the needs of the Church.

People used to have a tendency to reduce Christ to the limits of the sign which realized his presence, to think that he himself suffered whatever affected the sign in its materiality. So it often used to be said in France (and other countries) that one must not touch the Host with one's teeth, as if that could hurt Christ. Some people were rather worried about the fraction of the Host in the Mass. They no longer understood the meaning of this action, its sense of sharing and universality. There were hawked about for centuries accounts of miracles where Hosts bled in profane hands. These affecting tales had for the unbalanced all the attraction of sacrilege. What wounds Christ in attacks on the Host, is the hatred, and perhaps also the degradation of those who abandon themselves to this imbecile sorcery: it is not the physical, material character of what they do to the Host. Their outrages touch only the *sign,* the appearance, not the reality of the body of Christ. It is to that truth that the medieval hymns of the Blessed Sacrament had already given deep expression:

> The reality of God cannot be broken
> Only the sign is broken
> And in this breaking
> Neither the state nor the form of
>   what is signified
> Is made less

> *Nulla rei fit scissura*
> *Signi tantum fit fractura*
> *Qua nec status nec statura*
> *Signati minuitur.*

In short, in our understanding of the Eucharist as elsewhere, the present crisis is a crisis of growth, a purification, a return to what is essential, in spirit and in truth. It is the pursuit of the whole reality, the whole reality which the love of God has placed in the Eucharist. We are returning here to the doctrine of St. Thomas Aquinas which we have ignored. He explains that the real Presence does not mean that Christ suffers change in any way, or is "moved locally," moved in *place* or *space.* He remains in heaven, in that universal and universally communicable state which escapes the fragmentary duration of time. Only the bread and wine suffer the change which realizes his presence. And this change is not accessible to our eyes, or our touch, or to scientific instruments. It is wholly mysterious, beyond all appearances. That is why we call it a substantial change, that is to say a change which lies beneath what we can perceive, deeper in reality. Christ himself brings it about that the sign of bread, which is no longer bread but the appearance of bread, subsists, that is, continues to exist. He brings it about that the sign of wine, which is no longer wine, subsists. He makes them subsist as "pure" or mere signs of his presence. It is in this way that he is really present, but according to a spiritual, metaphysical mode whose nature is beyond our grasp.

It is here that the mystery of faith lies: that this Presence is completely real, but without on the one hand the body of Christ being in itself altered, and without on the other hand the series of natural causes which result in the characteristics of bread and wine being modified, "when we eat this bread and drink this cup."

This way of looking at the mystery is penetrating and fruitful. It makes manifest the divine wisdom. In giving himself God respects the natural order. His transcendent love does not debase itself in the ingenious metamorphoses of magic or mythology. It is in another order that he gives himself.

The teaching of St. Thomas Aquinas, so long ignored, has a double value.

It eliminates all disputes of a scientific kind, since the scientific order, the order of phenomena, is wholly respected on its own plane.

But above all it inculcates a more just, deeper, less unworthy idea of the way in which God gives himself to us. The unity of the risen Christ is not broken or changed. The consecration affects the bread, and not his body, which enters into a real and substantial relationship with the host. It is a matter then not so much of Christ "coming down upon the altar," as of an act by which he assumes, in "transubstantiating" them, the appearances of the oblation made on the altar. It is thus the whole community which is placed in contact with Christ in heaven and drawn by him and to him. So all the communities which celebrate Mass are assembled, beyond the diversities of time and place, in the person of Christ, in his unique sacrifice, more deeply even than many imagine. It is we who gravitate towards his Mystery rather than he towards our human affairs. We contact in this way the deep meaning of the liturgy as Eastern Christians are aware of it. For them the celebration of the Eucharist is less a descent of heaven upon earth as represented in the west, than an access to heaven, in anticipation, by the whole Christian community. It is eschatology already begun.

The coming of Christ among us, the rising of the Church towards him, these are only two complementary ways of talking about the same completely mysterious reality, the reality of the love of God, who gives himself to us.

If the mutation in man today obliges us to reflect, to *strip* our thought, it brings us back always, and definitively, to the essential reality, God's love for us and the response to which he invites us.

So we could take one by one all the dogmas which are in the process of being rethought, in the light of scripture and tradition and modern research, and we should see that the present "crisis" is essentially a vast effort to understand them more authentically and more fully. There are difficulties and hesitations, occasions when we have to grope and feel our way, tunnels we have to go through *en route,* but, in essence, what we are doing is returning to the authentic tradition beneath the approximations of the cultural language of the past, with which the intellectual rigor of the modern mind cannot be content. We are making manifest the full value of dogma for our time.

In every change something appears and something disappears. The grain of wheat sown in the earth dies in order to bear fruit. And we ask, "Is it germinating or is it rotting?" So a human mutation involves the disappearance of something: it implies a certain decomposition. And in mutations which fail there is only that. But in the present mutation all the indications are that we can say, "Life is germinating. It is being reborn." It is for each one of us to share in this rebirth, to hasten the time of the harvest.

Is It A Blessing To Believe?

VI IS IT A BLESSING TO BELIEVE?

Is it a blessing to believe? This is a subject for a thesis. Many books have been written on the blessing of faith.

Some people have not been convinced. They have the feeling faith is rather a nuisance, that it fetters them, that it stops them from doing what they want to do, that, in this world at least, it is not a matter for rejoicing. They would like to exploit in this sense the saying of St. Paul: "If Christ be not risen from the dead, then are we of all men most miserable" (1 Cor 15: 17-19).

This is to interpret the apostle's paradox wrongly. According to St. Paul, the misfortune would be, on this hypothesis, to be mistaken about the essential point. And every Christian worthy of the name will feel in the same way. To be deceived about the reality of his love, to love an illusion, this, to one who loves, is the greatest of all misfortunes.

But faith, taken seriously, is the source of a happiness which has been promised by Christ himself:

"Truly I say to you, there is no one who has left house or brothers or sisters or mother or father, or children or lands, for my sake and for the Gospel, who will not receive a hundred-fold *now in this time,*

houses and brothers, and sisters and mothers and lands
. . .' (Mk 10: 29-30).

Notice that it is not only in a post-terrestrial future
that Jesus promises this happiness. It is *now in this
time.*" He emphasizes this, lest we should make any
mistake about it. Anyone who takes his faith seriously
and gives up everything for God finds, in another way,
a way less exclusive and less possessive, a freer, and
more spiritual way, more generous and more shared,
the hundred-fold of what he would have had otherwise.
This was one of the elements in the radiant joy of
St. Francis, his earthly joy, which he had in brotherhood with all mankind, with all animals, with the whole
earth itself, of which he possessed not an inch in the
eyes of the world.

"Blessed be God for our sister water. . . ."

DOSTOEVSKY'S PARADOX

Some Christians have expressed the joy of faith
in strange and paradoxical terms:

"There is nothing better or more beautiful, nothing
deeper, nothing more reasonable or more sympathetic,
nothing more courageous, nothing more perfect than
Christ, and not only is there nothing, but I tell myself
with a jealous love there can be nothing. More than
that: if some one had proved to me that Christ is outside truth, and if, in reality, truth is outside Christ,
I would rather be with Christ than with truth."

This was how the famous novelist Dostoevsky

spoke at the end of 1884. And these are not the words of a man to whom faith came easily. The lines which precede them prove the contrary:

"I am a child of the age, of unbelief and doubt, right up to the present moment and even, I know, to the moment of death. What agony it has cost me, and costs me now, this thirst to believe, which is the stronger in my soul the more arguments there are in me against it. And yet God gives me moments when I am perfectly at peace. In these moments I love and find I am loved by others. It is in these moments that I have made for myself a creed in which everything is clear and sacred to me. And this creed is that there is nothing better or more beautiful than Christ."

It was in somewhat the same way that Fr. Valensin and his pupil François, who died very young, loved to repeat this passage from Fichte:

"If, impossibly, on my death bed, it were proved to me by irrefutable evidence that I had been wrong, that there is no life after death, that there is no God even, I should not be sorry that I had believed; I should think I had done myself honor in believing, and that if the universe is something foolish and contemptible, so much the worse for it, that the mistake was not in me, in that I believed that God is, but in God, that he was not" (A. Valensin, *François,* p. 166 and *Autour de ma foi,* p. 56, Paris, 1948).

Certainly if this just boiled down to saying, "I prefer my personal happiness to truth," or "I doubt my faith but I hang on to it because I find it congenial," it would be sordid and unsustainable. It would do injury

100

to Christ who is Truth. It would be a distressing inversion of spiritual values.

HE WHO SAVES HIS LIFE LOSES IT

But in fact it is something quite different. What these Christians are trying to say, paradoxically, is that Christ perceived and lived, is, of himself, a proof that nothing can go beyond: "I *am* Truth," he said. If, impossibly, another truth were to exist, they know that it could not compete with the truth they have received from God. St. Paul was no less paradoxical when he said, following in the footsteps of Moses (Ex 3:32):

"For I could wish that I myself were anathema, and cut off from Christ for the sake of my brethren" (Rm 9:3).

It is a cry, not a thesis; the words are winged, and if we try to tie them down, to *congeal* their meaning, we shall lose it, and the language will simply fall under the weight of its own import. It would have served no purpose at all, either for God or for men, that St. Paul should be damned. Quite the contrary. It was in another way that he saved his brethren.

What St. Paul is making clear, paradoxically, is that the happiness of the Christian is not an egotistical happiness, but the joy of a love which gives itself to the point of losing itself, and finds itself in losing itself: "He who wishes to save his life will lose it," said Christ, "and he who loses it will save it" (Mk 8: 35).

The joy of faith is not a static security, a tran-

quilizer against the agony of death. And yet we are in the hands of God, who cannot fail us. That means something, and man has not, and will never have, any other assurance in the face of death or in the face of certain kinds of solitude in this world.

In 1944, in my prisoner of war camp, I met an officer whom the easy pre-war days had carried a long way from God, and who found him again like this. He escaped. But he was recaptured by the Gestapo before he crossed the frontier. So he found himself, from one day to the next, alone, in close con-

finement, in a dark cell. There were no visits, no
companions, no interrogations. The only human contact was soup brought, once a day, without a word,
and from time to time the inquisitorial eye of the
guard, which he could suspect from a slight click behind the judas-hole. The guard used to come to see that
he was observing the rule: the prisoner was forbidden,
under pain of heavy sanctions, to lie down on his
straw mattress before curfew. He had no book, no
pencil or paper, no work, no distraction of any sort.
He thought he would go mad in this solitude, during
the long days and the interminable nights. And then
he found, in the depth of himself, a Presence. In the
fasting of his mind and body, the prayers of his childhood came back, he remembered verses of the Gospel,
words of the Mass that he thought he had forgotten.
He remembered them more every day, recovering them
slowly. He made the moments of grace last. He was
not alone, and that was why he "held out"... and also
why he deepened. When he came out, after about
a year, he was a different man, more a man and at the
same time a Christian.

SECURITY OR RISK?

The presence and love of God do bring security.
But perhaps we have insisted too much on this, to the
point of turning Christians into people who are "in-
sured," who recline inert on their ready-made security
as if it were a cushion, men of celestial property, who

Jesus did not promise happiness only in an other-worldly future but also here and now in this present life. He affirmed his promise with such insistence that there is no reason for us to deceive ourselves about it. He who takes his faith seriously will find in a different way—less exclusively and less possessively — the hundredfold of those who would possess the things of this world in an un-Christian fashion. In this sense, to believe is indeed a fortunate thing for he who believes is truly happier than he who has no faith.

"practice" Christianity as if it were a contract, without initiative or enthusiasm or love.

That is why talking about "the security of the faith" irritates certain Christians today to the point of anger. When friends said to Simone de Beauvoir, at the moment of her mother's death, "If you believed it would be a consolation to you," the prospect of such consolation seemed to her childish and dishonorable, a refuge from reality. And some committed Christians today are exceedingly hard on this cult of consolation. A French Dominican wrote recently:

"This is perhaps what we have to fight hardest against: the faith that is a consolation, the faith that without an experience of the precariousness of the world would have nothing to feed on, and according to which it would be through my losses and failures here that I should recover my outlay in the next. This is the opium of the people. . . . We are soaked in a kind of Christianity which makes for infantilism, in which we call to mind the consoling truths which render our existence tolerable" (J. Cardonnel, *Dieu est mort en Jésus-Christ,* Bordeaux, 1967, pp. 135-136).

WITH PERSECUTIONS

Real faith is seen as a risk, and it is in this sense that people talk about "the gamble of faith."

In the first place, to stake everything on faith, on the word of God, is to follow a sort of invisible

radar against the evidence of the senses—a stumbling block to Jews and a folly to pagans.

This is not accomplished without conflict, or without renouncing many of the securities of secular life.

107

In the early centuries, for instance, Christians had to give up the practice of certain professions in order to be baptized. One had to change one's whole way of life. And so still today, many people give up for the sake of the Gospel, a secure and established existence, a career which demands certain compromises, even if it be an ecclesiastical career. And again the promise of the hundred-fold is tied to a condition which is the very opposite of a security.

When he promised the hundred-fold in this world, Christ added, "with persecutions."

And elsewhere:

"Do not think that I have come to bring peace on earth; I have not come to bring peace but a sword. For I have come to set a man against his father, and a daughter against her mother, and a daughter-in-law against her mother-in-law; and a man's foes will be those of his own household" (Mt 19:34-36).

These words do not contradict the promise of Christmas: "Peace on earth to men whom God loves." They are situated at a different level. Peace is promised to whoever stakes everything on God and lives dangerously according to the demands of love. The peace of Christ is not always that of the world.

Our time is less than past centuries a time of static security for faith. Life in Christ will not survive without conversion. It is laborious and uncomfortable. One has ceaselessly to review one's life, one's formulas, and one's images, in the light of what the study of revelation manifests more clearly from day to day, and in the light of the demands of our age, always being renewed.

Today's security can no longer be that of a citadel or a stronghold. It is the security of the navigator, who knows how to adapt himself to the winds and tides. And this symbol of the Church is truer to the Gospels than the symbol of the stronghold.

It is then in allowing for all kinds of insecurity, both those about which Christ warned us and those which belong to the particular circumstances of our time, that faith will rediscover its "security," a dynamic security founded on the Gospel, a blessedness which is not the blessedness of this world, but that of the beatitudes, a security which is established in God.

Let it be in this sense then that we look for the blessing of faith. It is not to be sought in the image of the man who took the talent entrusted to him by his master and buried it, but in the man who used it to make more, in the merchant who sold all that he had to buy the pearl of great price or to buy the field where the hidden treasure lay. It is to be sought in the image of the grain of wheat which is sown in the ground and dies that it may bear fruit, in the image of Christ, who was not "attached to his divine condition as to a possession, but took upon himself the state of a servant" and all the risks of the human condition up to the heaviest, that of condemnation by Pontius

Pilate and the ignominious death on the cross. It is to those who follow him along this way that he gives the hundred-fold in this world.

THE IDEAL OF FAITH

With Christ who is the source and object of faith we must invoke her who is its example and model, who has best lived the condition of faith.

For Christ himself is in a certain sense beyond this condition, since he is himself the "Truth," the "light of the world." According to classical theology he seems not to have been immersed in the night which is characteristic of faith, although he experienced mysteriously in his human condition the darkness expressed by the words of his agony in Gethsemane or on the Cross: "My God, my God, why hast thou forsaken me?"

The Virgin Mary knew wholly, and as each one of us knows it, the common condition of faith. And that is the origin of her blessedness. "Blessed to have believed," said Elizabeth prophetically at the Visitation. She is not, like Christ, the source and object itself of faith, but wholly relative to faith.

On the word of God received at the Annunciation she staked her life, her reputation, her future, without knowing all the consequences. It was to God that she trusted herself. And so she was brought into the want and menace of Christ's existence, from the manger at Bethlehem to the foot of the Cross. The "blessing of faith" was for her as dark and painful as it can be

110

for a mother hurt in her maternal love by the death of an only son. She knew the hundred-fold of the Gospel's promise (Mk 10:30) but with the "persecutions" which are also promised, for her the "sword" of the Cross predicted by Simeon. It was in this ordeal that her faith became, in a definitive way, the very type and image of the faith of the Church vis-à-vis Christ. As the faith of the teaching Church is concentrated in the infallibility of the episcopal college, and can also be exercised by the pope alone, so the Blessed Virgin realized in her own person the infallibility of the Church taught, what is called *infallibilitas credendo,* the perfect receptiveness of faith lived.

May she help each of us to rediscover the secret which she has no greater desire than to share.

Easter—Christ's resurrection
and our own. In Christ
the resurrection was born
of suffering and death. For
us, Easter must be a search
to understand and to live
the gift of God, his grace,
in our life and in the world
today. Easter is not the
end of our journey but the
point of departure. It is
a program of spiritual renewal. Christ is our resurrection just as he is the
resurrection of the world.